In Search of
Christian Wisdom

Rediscovering
How Jesus Taught

In Search of
Christian Wisdom

Rediscovering
How Jesus Taught

WILLIAM A. HERR

THE THOMAS MORE PRESS
Chicago, Illinois

ISBN 0-88347-221-x

CONTENTS

This book had its origin in a lecture delivered at Newman House, on the campus of Southern Illinois University, at the invitation of Rev. Jack Frerker.

Its themes were developed and refined during a week-long seminar conducted at Mount Mary College, Milwaukee, at the invitation of Sister Sandra Ann Weinke, SSND, and Sister Mary Hester Valentine, SSND.

Introduction

ONCE upon a time there was a man who had reached the advanced age of forty without ever having been married. Then one day he found a woman who seemed absolutely ideal. She was beautiful, she was intelligent, she was warm and sincere, and she had a wonderful sense of humor. She had everything, in fact; and the man was convinced that at last he had found the right woman for him. There was only one problem: the woman in question insisted that she did not believe in love.

Now the woman had some excellent reasons for feeling this way. But the man did not see how he would be able to establish a close and lasting relationship with someone who considered the very idea of love impossible. And so, since he knew that the woman was religious, he devised what he thought was an exceptionally ingenious stratagem. One day, when all his other arguments had failed, he played his trump card. "How can

William A. Herr

you believe in God," he asked her with an air of triumph, "and not believe in love?"

We need not concern ourselves with the details of what happened next, except to say that the man and the woman eventually were married and began to live happily ever after.

The epilogue to this story is that, about a week later, the man was sitting in a restaurant, thinking about something else entirely, when suddenly he realized that the question which he has asked cut both ways. How could he—clever fellow that he thought he was—how could he believe in love without also believing in God?

The implications of that question led, eventually, to the writing of this book.

Religious faith does indeed have a great deal in common with love, and this fact provides an excellent starting point for an inquiry into the way in which the Christian faith traditionally has been presented in the Roman Catholic Church. This inquiry will help us to understand why Jesus taught in the way that he did, and also to appreciate some of what was lost when those to whom he entrusted his church adopted teaching methods different from his own.

Jesus himself insisted that the essence of the Christian religion is love. If someone were to ask what it means to be a Catholic, however, most people's first reaction probably would not be to say that Catholics are people who love the Lord their God with their whole hearts, and souls, and minds, and strengths, and who love their neighbors as themselves. Most people would be far more likely to reply that Catholics are people who believe in papal primacy and apostolic succession and the doctrine of the Immaculate Conception.

It is clear that something has changed since the time of Jesus. As a matter of fact, a great many things have changed. There has been, down through the centuries, a profound shift of emphasis within the Catholic tradition away from the actual teachings of Jesus and toward the formulation of doctrinal propositions—away from the spirit of the Sermon on the Mount, as it were, and toward the spirit of the Syllabus of Errors.

More specifically, there has been for many hundreds of years an over-emphasis upon theology—defined, for purposes of this discussion, as theoretical knowledge about God—at the expense of religion, or the cultivation of a personal commitment to and a personal union with God.

This volume will examine some of the factors which brought about this change of orientation, and it will trace some of the consequences of that change. It will explore the possibility of developing a different method of Christian intellectual inquiry, one which could serve as an alternative to formal theological systems on the one hand and to literal, unquestioning fundamentalism on the other: a method which would proceed by drawing out what already is present inside each person rather than by formulating abstract propositions for him or her to accept.

It also will suggest, finally, that Catholic educational and pastoral activities should concentrate less than they traditionally have upon transmitting theology and more upon cultivating religion—that they should imitate much more closely than they have in the past, in other words, the teaching techniques which Jesus himself employed.

CHAPTER ONE
Commitment vs. Assent

WE ALL know that Jesus did not come to earth to transmit theoretical knowledge. He did not give those to whom he preached a set of answers or a theological system. Like the other great religious teachers of history, he communicated his message, for the most part, through parables, allegories, and figures of speech.

Jesus did not ask those to whom he preached to agree with him, but to follow him: to try to establish the same relationship with God which he himself enjoyed. He was far less concerned with theology than he was with religion, far more interested in how people lived than in what they believed.

One reason why Jesus used allegories so frequently is that religious language is by its very nature allegorical— or, if one prefers, analogical. It has more in common with poetry than with logic. It is suggestive and ambiguous, not analytical, because it refers to a reality which surpasses the limits of human understanding. Religious language, like religion itself, is primarily concerned with establishing and strengthening personal union with God.

Another reason why Jesus taught by means of parables and allegories rather than by constructing logical arguments is that he was trying to transform people's lives. He was encouraging them to make a total and unconditional act of religious faith, a process in which logic can play little part because it involves far more than intellectual assent: it requires a personal commitment.

This point is of supreme importance, but it often is glossed over by those who try to make religious faith more palatable by implying that faith in God is similar to faith that the earth is round or to faith that there actually was such a person as Alexander the Great.

Arguments like these, however, really trivialize religious faith. To believe that the earth is round is merely to assent to a factual proposition. Assertions of this kind may interest me, but they do not involve me personally. I may agree that they are true or insist that they are false, but in neither case do I need to do anything about them. My agreement or disagreement does not cause anything to change.

This is not the kind of faith which Kierkegaard had in mind when he wrote about "fear and trembling," and it is not the kind of faith which made possible Simon Peter's scandalous answer to that terrifying question, "Who do *you* say that I am?"

The difference between personal commitment and intellectual assent is reflected in the difference between saying "I love chocolate" and saying "I love you."

"I love chocolate" is a simple statement of fact. It does not imply any commitment on my part, or any further consequences of any kind. Someone who says "I love you" to another person, on the other hand, and then walks away as though nothing of importance had happened, as though that statement did not create or reinforce some type of bond between him or her and the person addressed, simply does not understand what those words mean.

The same is true of religious faith. "I believe that the earth is round" is a statement which I can make on a purely intellectual level. It does not imply any commitment. When the apostle Thomas fell to his knees and cried out, "My Lord and my God," however, he was not merely assenting to a factual proposition. He was making a religious statement, not a theological one. He was committing himself to Jesus, making an act of the will which changed the orientation of his entire life.

A profession of love which does not change anything of importance is not really a profession of love, and an act of faith which changes nothing cannot truly be an act of religious faith.

Because we tend to overlook the importance of personal commitment, we often think of faith in terms of assent to a formal creed—as equivalent to orthodoxy, as the opposite of heresy—rather than in terms of a response to God. If a person declares that he or she believes in "God, the Father Almighty, creator of heaven and earth, and in Jesus Christ, his only son, Our Lord," and assents to other traditional formulas, we are apt to conclude, on this basis alone, that such a person does indeed "have the faith."

Agreement with a set of propositions, however, never has constituted personal commitment. It is quite possible that many of those who have given their full and complete assent to the formal creeds never have made a mature, deliberate personal decision to surrender themselves to God.

We even speak of a person's being "born into the faith," as though faith could be inherited like the color of one's eyes. True faith, however, cannot be passed on from one person to another, from teacher to pupil or from parent to child or from priest to parishioner, in the same way that factual knowledge can. Faith requires a commitment which each person must make for himself or herself and it must be cultivated in, created anew by, drawn forth from, each separate individual.

Because it involves commitment, love of one person for another rests upon a choice. I have little control, if any, over whom I am attracted to; but I do have control over whom I choose to make commitments to, and whether or not I choose to make commitments to anyone at all.

Religious faith also is a choice, which means that it depends more upon the will than on the intellect. The ultimate reason why we believe is simply that we have decided that we would do so. No one can argue anyone into loving someone else, and faith does not follow logically from any syllogism. Knowledge of certain facts may make the faith decision easier, but no amount of knowledge can compel it in the way that knowledge of arithmetic compels one to agree that three plus two equals five. If the evidence for our religious beliefs really were conclusive in and of itself, we would have no need for faith.

It is true that many people say that they believe in God because of evidence of one sort or another—the complexities of nature, perhaps, or the order of the universe. But if one were to ask such a person what evidence he or she would accept as proving that God does *not* exist, it would become apparent very quickly that his or her faith, like all religious faith, rests not upon empirical data but upon a decision to believe. First we choose, then we find evidence to support that choice. This is not insincerity; it is just the nature of faith and of love.

No logical argument can prove that anyone should make either of these choices, because they both require commitments which go far beyond what the evidence at hand appears to justify. Much of the evidence which supports these commitments is encountered only after the commitments have been made.

One must make the choice to accept or not accept another person, and to offer or not to offer oneself for his or her acceptance, without knowing in advance how that person will respond. Anyone who insists on certainty ahead of time will simply never make a love commitment.

In the same way, only those who have made the leap of religious faith really can be sure that their faith rests upon a firm foundation. They know it because they have experienced it, but they cannot prove it to anyone else. The most that they can do is to suggest to others how they might find out for themselves.

The same is true for certain other kinds of faith. Some people choose to believe that goodness will triumph over evil, and kindness over cruelty, and honesty over deceit, and persist in those beliefs despite all contrary evidence. Some people choose to remain faithful to their spouses or to religious vows, even though other people consider such commitments foolish.

Those who make decisions such as these are making acts of faith, just as surely as the apostle Thomas did. Their choices go beyond what human reason can ascertain. They transcend reason, just like the commitment which Jesus asked his followers to make.

The choice of whether to open or not to open myself to someone else's love is more than a decision about another person: it is a decision about myself as well. It is part of the process of determining what kind of person I will be and what kind of life I will lead. To open or not to open oneself to an acknowledgment of God is a decision with similar implications.

This is one reason why choices such as faith and love entail extraordinary risk. If I should make a poor investment—if I should buy a certain stock, let us say, just before it drops in value—my mistake would be a factual one. It would be like thinking that the sun will shine on a particular day, and then having it rain while I am waxing my car. Making a wrong decision where the stock market is concerned would affect my monetary worth, but not my human worth.

William A. Herr

If I entrust myself to someone, on the other hand, and if that trust should be betrayed, I will experience a different kind of loss. I would have risked not merely my money but my human worth; and I would have been not merely impoverished but made a fool of.

All my dignity would have been stripped away. The ground would have been cut out from under me—as it would have been for Simon Peter, if, after having openly proclaimed Jesus to be the son of the living God, he had discovered that Jesus was, in fact, a fraud. The possibility that one might be mistaken in a matter such as this is indeed a cause for fear and trembling.

And yet, while I never can be absolutely certain that the one to whom I am about to offer myself will accept me, or that the religious commitment which I am about to make is not based upon a delusion, it is possible to be certain that I am justified in offering myself for another's acceptance or in making religious commitments.

Nothing can remove the risks from love—or from faith. It may be possible to demonstrate, however, that both are risks worth taking.

CHAPTER TWO

Responding to God's Invitation

ALTHOUGH love depends upon a choice, that choice is not an arbitrary one. Accepting others, and offering ourselves for their acceptance, is a basic, universal human need. It is part of our humanity, and we can deny it only by denying who and what we are. If we persist in this denial, we close off a part of us, not just from others, but from ourselves as well. No one can lead a happy and fulfilling life unless he or she is open to the possibility of love.

Since a desire for love is intrinsic to our nature, loving should be natural and easy for us. It is the way we all would act toward one another if nothing hindered us from doing so, and all that is required to enable us to love is to eliminate whatever may be keeping us from loving—just as one gains happiness by removing those things which are making him or her unhappy.

The most effective means of enabling ourselves to love is simply love itself. Making a decision to accept

William A. Herr

another opens up the possibility of being accepted in return, and being accepted by another helps remove the fear which was keeping us from making the decision. Conversely, only after we accept ourselves can we allow another to accept us—but the knowledge that another is willing to accept us can help us to accept ourselves. Something similar can occur with faith: "I do believe; help thou my unbelief."

Sometimes, however, we may not be able to accomplish this alone. Opening ourselves to love requires us to abandon our self-centeredness and our delusions of self-sufficiency. It means acknowledging our weaknesses and inadequacies, and it means being willing to reveal our inner selves to others. It may mean having to look at things inside ourselves which we have never dared to face. Loving means surrender, which may not come easily.

Fear of making the act of self-surrender which love demands may make us strike out at those who insist upon accepting us when we cannot accept ourselves. It may make us flee in panic, without even knowing why we run—like the protagonist of Francis Thompson's "The Hound of Heaven," who

... fled him, down the nights and down the days;
I fled him, down the arches of the years;

IN SEARCH OF CHRISTIAN WISDOM

I fled him, down the labyrinthine ways
Of my own mind. . . .

Fear, however, does not remove our need for love. It merely forces us to seek its satisfaction in strange and sometimes self-destructive ways.

Fear may cause us to try to make ourselves believe that we can get along without love, or that we are incapable of loving, or even that there is nothing in us which anyone could love. And, if we work long and hard enough, we may convince ourselves that it is true.

And yet someone who knew us, and who cared about us, might not accept this judgment. Since the need for love is universal, this person would feel confident that, on this point at least, he or she could judge our situation better than we ourselves could.

Such a person might try to show us that love already is part of our everyday experience, and that each of us is, in fact, the beneficiary of many people's acceptance and concern, whether we wish to be or not. He or she might try to help us realize that our very existence presupposes love.

Sometimes people with an unusually strong fear of love can be helped to overcome this fear through a kind of dialogue which draws out and makes explicit what is hidden deep within them.

William A. Herr

This type of dialogue does not aim at persuasion, but at revelation. It is a technique for helping people to accept things which they have been unwilling or unable to confront, and to discover the significance of those things for themselves. It tries to bring people into contact and harmony with themselves, so that they will be able to lower the self-erected barriers which are keeping them from accepting what they so desperately need and want.

Although this kind of dialogue deals with irrational subject matter, the dialogue itself has a rational structure; and it is effective because there is an objective basis for it. It is a systematic search for self-knowledge —for only through acknowledgment of who we are can we arrive at self-acceptance. This includes acknowledgment of the fact that we are not self-sufficient, that we cannot achieve our happiness and self-fulfillment all by ourselves.

Faith requires similar acknowledgments.

In a sense, then, love can be induced. It can be drawn out of people by helping them identify and overcome the obstacles which frustrate their natural striving for it. Another person can help to prepare us for loving by leading us to the point where nothing hinders us from choosing to love except our own decision not to choose it. Another person can help us return to a condition in which loving and trusting come naturally to us—which is another way of saying that he or she can help us become again as little children.

If one person can help another to remove the barriers which are keeping him or her from giving and accepting love, then the same thing should be possible with respect to faith.

That such preparation sometimes is required is shown in many passages of Scripture. Some of those to whom Jesus preached, for example, did not respond because "their hearts were hardened." The Gospel compares the Kingdom of Heaven to seed, some of which withered and died because it fell upon hard ground, ground which had not been made ready for it.

It is true that we cannot give ourselves the gift of faith, or give it to another, any more than we can bring love into existence merely by wishing for it. The most that anyone can do is to try to make certain that he or she will be receptive if the occasion for real love or faith should present itself.

Although no amount of reasoning can compel an act of faith, one may be able to help others to become more amenable to such an act, should God choose to let the seed of faith fall on that particular ground. There are several ways in which this could be done.

Reason can help someone realize that the attitude

which he or she takes toward religious faith is a matter
of supreme importance. This is more or less what
Pascal was trying to accomplish with his famous analogy of the wager.

Let us say, Pascal proposed, that there is only one
chance in a hundred million that the God whom Jesus
called "Father" actually exists. Even then, there would
be one chance in a hundred million of gaining infinite
happiness if we commit ourselves to such a God, and
no chance at all if we do not. Should even that one single chance be cast away without investigation? This, of
course, is not an argument for God's existence; it is an
argument for taking the possibility of God's existence
seriously.

Reason may be able to help people who fear to choose
the kind of commitment which religious faith requires
because that choice, like all choices, eliminates the possibility of choosing certain other things. Again, in Francis Thompson's words,

For, though I knew His love
Who followed,
Yet I was sore adread,
Lest, having Him, I must have naught beside

IN SEARCH OF CHRISTIAN WISDOM

Although such fears are, in fact, well-founded, reason should be able to demonstrate that whatever we may have to lose by opening ourselves to love or to faith is inconsequential, compared to what we certainly will lose if we refuse to do so.

Reason also can make clear that the choice of whether or not to respond to God's invitation cannot be avoided. If we do not open ourselves to the possibility of faith, then by that very fact we are closing ourselves to it, just as if a man should ask a woman to marry him, and she should refuse to respond to his proposal, she would in fact be rejecting it. Not choosing, as has frequently been observed, is itself a choice.

Reason can even help to prepare a person to accept religious faith by demonstrating reason's own limitations.

If it is indeed the case that God is the foundation and presupposition of our very existence, then reason should be able to reveal evidence of that fact—not absolute proof, but evidence: "footprints of God," to use St. Bonaventure's phrase. It is true that this evidence can be recognized as evidence only through the eyes of faith, but it is also true that it probably will not be recognized at all by those who are not prepared to encounter it.

William A. Herr

If a friend should tell us that he or she had looked everywhere for love and could not find it, how would we respond? We probably would reply, in one manner or another, that love is not something outside oneself, like a golden nugget or other precious object, which can be discovered and possessed if only one searches carefully enough. It is, rather, something which already is within us, waiting for an opportunity to express itself, something inherent and implicit in each person's experience, which we must merely acknowledge and accept.

Brooker T. Washington once told the story of a sailing ship which had been lost for many days upon the ocean and had exhausted its water supplies. Then one day the lookout spotted another ship; and the captain sent a signal, "We need fresh water." The other ship, however, signaled back, "Lower your buckets right where you are."

The first ship repeated its message, "We need fresh water; we are dying of thirst." But the other ship sent back the same answer, "Lower your buckets right where you are." Again and again the two ships exchanged the same messages.

Finally, in desperation, the captain of the first ship ordered his crew to lower buckets into the sea, and they drew up fresh, sparkling water.

The lost ship had drifted near the coast of Brazil, and

IN SEARCH OF CHRISTIAN WISDOM

was floating upon an immense stream of fresh water extending far out into the Atlantic from the mouth of the Amazon River. The captain and his crew had been suffering the agonies of death by thirst while floating upon the very thing that they were thirsting for, but they needed someone else to help them recognize it for what it was.

Would we not give the same reply to a friend who asked where he or she should look for love? Would we not tell that person, "Stop running and stop searching —lower your buckets right where you are?"

And if someone were to say that he or she was willing to accept the reality of God, if only he or she could find evidence of it, we might give the same reply: "Lower your buckets right where you are." God, we might say, like love, need not be sought but only recognized and acknowledged.

We may already possess all we need in order to believe, but we may not realize it. Perhaps the kingdom of heaven is indeed within us, if only we were conscious of it. Perhaps we merely need to become aware of and accept the implications of things which we already know.

If so, then reason can help to bring us face to face with the choice which must be made and help to focus our attention on it.

This is the approach which Ignatius of Loyola is said

William A. Herr

to have utilized to help bring about the conversion of Francis Xavier. (I am indebted for this story to Sister Mary Hester Valentine.) Instead of preaching or arguing, instead of trying to teach him something which he did not already know, Loyola utilized a form of rational dialogue to draw out of Xavier a response which Xavier was forced to acknowledge as valid and authentic because it was merely the explicit expression of something of which he already was implicitly aware.

Ignatius began by asking Francis what he planned to do with his life, and Francis replied that he intended to finish his education.

"Yes," replied Ignatius, "and then what?"

Francis answered that then he wanted to go into business and earn a great amount of money.

"Yes," replied Ignatius, "and then what?"

Francis answered that then he planned to marry a girl from a good family and have children.

"Yes," replied Ignatius, "and then what?"

Francis, becoming somewhat flustered, answered that he planned to enjoy his prosperity and his family and live to a ripe old age.

"Yes," replied Ignatius, "and then what?"

After a pause, Francis answered reluctantly that once his allotted years had expired, he would die.

"Yes," replied Ignatius, "and then what?"

CHAPTER THREE

Transcendence in the Commonplace

JESUS, of course, was aware of all of this. He understood that people generally experience religious transformations not when they acquire new information, but when they achieve a deeper understanding of things which they already knew but whose full significance they had not yet realized.

For this reason Jesus tried to help his followers to become aware of the religious implications of the commonplace events in their everyday lives, thereby turning each of these events into a revelation of God and an encounter with him. He did not concentrate on teaching people new things but on helping them perceive a new dimension of things, a dimension which many of them might otherwise never have focused on.

Jesus also understood that one becomes truly and personally committed to something by realizing its truth for oneself, rather than by merely agreeing with what someone else has said. As John Shea has expressed it in his book *The Spirit Master:*

William A. Herr

The disciple must experience the teaching physically and spiritually. . . . (Jesus) wants the disciple to experience the reality he (Jesus) knows; he does not want to pass along the conclusions of his (own) experience. In the deepest moment it is not a sharing of belief and theology, but an introduction to Abba.

The faith commitment must be drawn out of a person as a response to that person's own interior experience; it cannot be imposed upon him or her.

That is why Jesus so frequently taught by means of religious parables, which are a means of helping people to discover for themselves some aspect of their relationship with God. A well-constructed parable gradually leads those to whom it is addressed to the point where they achieve a religious insight—to the point where they come to a new or deeper realization of some religious truth—and then encourages them to act upon that insight.

This is comparable to the way in which skillful parents sometimes teach by creating situations in which their children come to an understanding of something by thinking it out for themselves.

Since parables are religious rather than theological discourse, their content cannot be rigidly or precisely defined. Unlike theological statements, parables are neither true nor false. Was there really, literally, a Good Samaritan, or a Prodigal Son, or a Widow's Mite? The correct answer to such questions is neither "yes" nor "no" nor "maybe," but rather "it doesn't make any difference."

The significance of a parable lies not in the information which it conveys but in the invitation which it extends and in the response which it demands. The real message of the parable of the Good Samaritan was quite simple: "A certain man treated a total stranger as though he were his own brother. Now, what are YOU going to do?"

At this point the listener must make a choice about what kind of person he or she wants to be—whether he or she will accept the invitation to follow Jesus and live as he himself lived. This is similar in some respects to the situation of a man or woman who must decide whether or not to acknowledge his or her love for another person and surrender to it. What kind of orientation does he or she wish to adopt toward life, one of openness and acceptance or one of coldness and rejection? Will he or she respond to the grace which has been offered, or turn his or her back on it?

Parables are more effective in encouraging interior commitment than proofs or exhortations are, precisely because they call for this kind of personal decision. The parables of Jesus, like Jesus himself, did not say "agree with me," but "follow me." They attempted to move the listener, not by proceeding from step to logical step toward the demonstration of some abstract proposition, but by appealing directly to the judgment of his or her better self.

Jesus, through his parables, tried to reach and call forth something which he believed lay within the hearts of his listeners, even though they themselves did not yet realize it. He had confidence that what he was trying to reach really existed, not because those to whom he preached were saintly, or heroic, or exceptional in any other way, but simply because they were human beings. He knew that everyone has fundamental and undeniable spiritual needs, just as everyone has a fundamental and undeniable need for love.

A critic once wrote that Giuseppe Verdi had the ability to compose music which, when we hear it for the first time, it seems that we have known it all our lives. The words of Jesus seem to have had a similar effect on those who were prepared to receive them.

Some people, after hearing him speak only once, immediately abandoned everything they had and followed him. These people were not persuaded; they were attracted. Jesus was not the kind of messiah whom they had been expecting, but they recognized him nonetheless. There was something in his words which induced them to make a radical change in the orientation of their lives. He taught them a different way to live, and a different way to pray, and a different way of understanding their relationship with God.

His teachings were accepted, not because he proved that they were true with intellectual arguments, but because they were apprehended as true by his listeners' hearts—which, to borrow a phrase of Pascal, had reasons of their own which their reason did not know. He did not try to prove the truth of what he taught, because its truth was self-evident. He merely tried to help people to realize for themselves how self-evident it was.

Jesus brought his listeners into contact with God; and those whose hearts were receptive were drawn toward God; and they followed Jesus because they recognized God in him. This, in the most fundamental sense, is how Jesus taught.

It appears that the earliest Christian communities generally followed this example. Their faith utterances were not dogmas but statements of praise and gratitude and acknowledgments of Jesus as Lord. Like "I love you," these utterances expressed a personal commitment; and, by verbalizing that commitment, they strengthened it.

For many early Christians, expressions of this kind

William A. Herr

were quite sufficient—as, indeed, they are for many Christians today. It is true, as Aristotle pointed out, that all people by nature desire to know; but it also is true that there are many different ways of knowing, and that not everyone feels a need to engage in abstract speculation.

As time went on, however, those who were not content simply to live the Christian message but also wished to comprehend it as completely as possible— those who were not satisfied with "it's a mystery" in response to their questions—took the first steps toward creating a specifically Christian type of theoretical knowledge.

Some of these people found it necessary to explain or defend their beliefs; others merely wished to satisfy their own desire to understand. Whatever their motives, all of them sought Christian answers to questions which Christ himself had not found it necessary to address.

Scripture, for example, refers to Jesus as the Son of God. Does this mean that Jesus also was God? If so, is there more than one God? Was the mother of Jesus also the mother of God? If so, did she bring God into the world? Was she, in that case, a goddess herself? If Jesus was the only-begotten Son of God, was there a time before he was begotten when he did not exist?

IN SEARCH OF CHRISTIAN WISDOM

Questions such as these cannot be answered until one has determined what it means to be God, which means that any attempt to answer them is an attempt to understand and express something which by definition surpasses all understanding and expression. It also, of course, has nothing whatsoever to do with feeding the hungry, or sheltering the homeless, or loving one's neighbor as oneself.

We are built in such a way that we can understand something new only by relating it to something which we already know. For intellectually-minded persons in the early centuries of the Christian era, relating Christianity to what they already knew meant trying to comprehend it within the framework of the only systematic body of knowledge with which they were familiar, the writings of the Greek philosophers.

This body of knowledge, which included such disciplines as physics, biology, political science, astronomy, jurisprudence, and psychology, was almost coextensive with human reason itself for most of the educated citizens of the Roman Empire. No one spent much time worrying about whether or not those were the most appropriate intellectual structures to use, because they were the only ones available at the time.

To utilize Greek philosophy to try to understand Christianity meant incorporating the teachings of Jesus

William A. Herr

into a pre-existing and pagan way of looking at the world but at that particular moment in history the only alternative was not to try to understand it at all. This would have required educated Christians to totally separate their intellectual and their religious lives, to embrace some form of extreme religious fundamentalism.

The question of what attitude Christianity should take toward reason in general, and toward the teachings of the pagan Greek philosophers in particular, was not decided in any formal or official manner. No general council debated it. Instead, a consensus gradually emerged as the result of countless individual disputes between bishops, priests, and laypeople with conflicting viewpoints.

Tertullian, for example, who was born about a century and a half after Jesus, argued strenuously and eloquently that the knowledge which comes with faith is so much more perfect, more certain, and more sublime than the knowledge produced by human reason that reason has little if anything to say about religious matters. Where faith and reason are in harmony, reason is not necessary; and where they are in conflict, it must be rejected.

Not only will logic not lead one to God, Tertullian believed, it can be a positive hindrance: any teacher other than Jesus himself can only lead us away from the

IN SEARCH OF CHRISTIAN WISDOM

path which Jesus wishes us to follow. "What has Athens (reason) to do with Jerusalem (faith)?" he asked. Why should Christians read philosophical works when the Holy Spirit communicates directly to the church through prophets?

If this view had prevailed, the great Christian theological systems never would have been constructed but ultimately it did not prevail. Clement of Alexandria, a contemporary of Tertullian, was only one of the many writers who insisted that faith and reason cannot possibly be opposed, because there is only one wisdom and one truth, whether it be found in the Bible or in the works of Greek metaphysicians.

Reason, Clement taught, is God's greatest gift to humanity; and by its very nature it tends to lead all sincere inquirers to God. Systematic reasoning, in fact, serves to prepare an unbeliever's mind to accept the teachings of Christ, just as the Law of Moses was intended to prepare the Jews to accept it. Furthermore, once one has accepted Christianity, he or she should make every effort to comprehend its meaning. As Clement expressed it, "I believe in order that I might understand."

In the end, the legitimacy of using human reason to clarify and expound the basic tenets of Christianity, to some degree at least, was almost universally accepted—

especially among educated people, who tended, as always, to be the only ones in a position to make their views widely known.

Even Tertullian, who insisted that philosophy has nothing whatsoever to do with Christianity and that everything of value in the writings of the Greeks had been stolen from the Hebrew scriptures, was forced to construct logical arguments to defend his position.

As different thinkers took different philosophical presuppositions as starting-points for their speculations, they developed a variety of formal systems: intellectual structures which utilized technical language and metaphysical principles—and, eventually, logical analysis—to specify and clarify what Christianity really means.

Just as contemporary scholars attempt to relate *Genesis* to the findings of modern geology and cosmology or try to determine how psychiatry can help us to understand the miracles of Jesus, so Christian writers began to investigate such questions as how the neoplatonic theory of emanation could be used to explain the process of creation and the relationship of the different persons of the Trinity, and how various gospel passages should be interpreted in view of Plato's teaching that our bodies and the entire physical world are only reflections of higher and more perfect realities.

The question which remained to be answered, however, was what role these formal systems should play in the lives of individual Christians, and what relation they were to have to the actual teachings of Christ. Were they to be understood as one way among many of approaching the Christian message, or as the dominant one?

It is one thing for Christianity to have an intellectual life; it is something quite different for it to have no other life but an intellectual one. It is all well and good for reason to be utilized in the service of faith, but it is neither well nor good for rational concepts to be looked upon as equally important as, or even as a substitute for, an individual's personal relationship with and commitment to God.

CHAPTER FOUR

The Stranglehold of Formulas

THE use of philosophical concepts to supplement the knowledge which is revealed in scripture and obtained through personal religious experience gave rise to Christian "theology," the anglicized form of a Greek word which can be translated as "discourse about God," or "knowledge about God," or even "the study of God." This had profound effects upon the subsequent development of Christianity, not all of which were beneficial.

Christian apologists who utilized the methods and terminology of the Greek philosophers also tended to adopt those philosophers' conception of truth as something which is absolutely certain and eternal. They sought to construct propositions which would express the essential beliefs of Christianity in an unchanging manner—abstract universal truths, rather than expressions of what each of us as an individual has chosen to commit himself or herself to.

These propositions were intended to transmit a precisely defined factual content not only to contemporaries but also to generations yet unborn, more or less like any other body of factual information. This, as we have seen, was the precise opposite of the approach which Jesus used.

As more and more emphasis was placed upon theoretical knowledge, less was placed upon personal union with God. This had the effect of encouraging Christians to look upon God as an object to be learned about from teachers or textbooks, rather than as a person to be encountered and loved. The church itself, meanwhile, grew suspicious of non-intellectual sources of knowledge—such as mysticism and all other forms of personal experience of the divine—which could not be reduced to unequivocal formulas and subjected to logical analysis.

Theology increasingly became a substitute for religious experience rather than a reflection upon that experience, and in the process it cut itself off from its own roots. To quote John Shea once again:

Theological activity is a second-order activity. It presupposes more primary religious experiences which have generated faith perspectives and values. Theology explores and extends these perspectives and values into all the areas of human life. . . . Without a

William A. Herr

"sense of salvation" which the religious experience provides, theology becomes abstract, ideological, and insensitive. . . .

The creation of a body of abstract theological knowledge, and the privileged position which church leaders soon began to accord to that body of knowledge, also tended to turn Christianity itself into something like an academic discipline, whose safekeeping was entrusted to an elite group of specialists. Almost the only role which remained for the non-specialists—which eventually included virtually all of the laity, male and female alike—was to give their assent to the conclusions which these specialists had reached.

This assent usually was given through the recitation of creeds, or officially sanctioned summaries of theological conclusions. As time went on, more attention began to be paid to the precise wording of these formulas than to the inner sentiments of which they were supposed to be the expression.

By the middle of the fourth century, for example, such extraordinary significance had become attached to formal doctrinal statements that it was customary for the entire congregation to listen intently while neophytes recited their baptismal creed, in order to make certain that not a single word would be omitted or changed—as though the perpetuation of Christianity depended upon the accurate transmission of a particular sequence of syllables rather than upon the cultivation of a particular kind of religious commitment in people's hearts.

Creeds, in other words, already were being looked upon as being the Christian faith, rather than merely as ritualized expressions of it. In time, people tended to look upon Christianity itself as a set of propositions to be accepted and assented to on the basis of arguments and proofs, not a way of integrating one's own inner experiences which is accepted because it is intuitively recognized as valid by particular individuals.

Repetition of dogmatic formulas, however, does not increase one's personal commitment to God in the same way that the faith utterances of the early Christians did. We know things with our heads, but we make commitments with our hearts and the heart expresses itself most fully and most truly when it speaks without a prepared script.

Since theological statements usually are expressed in precise technical terms, they contain none of the ambiguity and subjectivity which is characteristic of faith utterances and other religious language. They also are understood to logically exclude the truth of their contradictories—which means that if two people disagree

William A. Herr

about the truth of a particular theological proposition, at least one of them must be objectively wrong. As a result, the development of traditional theology opened the door to nearly twenty weary centuries of anathemas and excommunications.

This stands in sharp contrast to the case of religious language, where the most extravagant and wildly conflicting expressions can coexist quite easily with one another, like flowers in a garden or the designs on a patchwork quilt, each making its own unique contribution to a total effect which no one of them could produce by itself.

By removing subjectivity and ambiguity, theological language made it much easier to focus upon the relatively few differences between the ways in which various Christians expressed their faith commitments rather than upon the far more numerous respects in which those expressions resembled one another. Eventually, Christian theologians were attacking each other's beliefs far more viciously than their predecessors had attacked paganism.

(Some insight into the differences between theological knowledge and the knowledge which flows from personal religious experience, and into the kinds of tragic consequences which can ensue when the two come into conflict with one another, may be obtained by examining what transpired when the theologians of the Inquisition were called upon to judge the orthodoxy of mystics. One can only presume, and hope, that the mystics would have judged the theologians more leniently.)

The practice of trying to apply the logical implications of human concepts to God led to particularly serious consequences when theologians extended their speculations to issues which the gospel writers did not address—problems, in fact, of which it would have been almost impossible for them to conceive.

It led to even more serious consequences when theologians began to insist that one specific metaphysical formula rather than another must be used to express some aspect of the divine reality, despite the fact that it is not written anywhere in scripture that one must embrace a particular metaphysical school in order to follow Christ.

It led to absolute catastrophe when theologians began trying to impose their conclusions upon those who disagreed with them, sometimes seeking the assistance of the secular government to make certain that their views prevailed. This had the effect of turning differences of opinion over theological formulations into affairs of state, and of encouraging secular rulers to involve themselves in those differences.

William A. Herr

The first attempt at imposing a particular theological proposition by force was made only a few years after Christians gained freedom of worship. In the year 325, emperor Constantine determined to put an end to a conflict between supporters and opponents of the Egyptian presbyter Arius by convening a church council in his palace in Nicaea. During the course of this council, Constantine instructed the bishops who were present to adopt a formal creed which declared that God the Son is "consubstantial" with God the Father— a technical term derived from Greek metaphysics.

Many bishops opposed the idea of making a technical definition of the relationship between the Father and the Son into an article of faith, since it is not contained in scripture. They also objected to using the word "consubstantial," which could be interpreted to mean that the Son is identical to the Father, or that they had a common origin, or that they both are material beings.

All but a few of the bishops at Nicaea eventually endorsed the use of "consubstantial," particularly after Constantine threatened to depose those who refused. They realized, however, that in going beyond scripture they were taking an unprecedented step; and they stated quite explicitly that they did not intend that their actions should serve as an example for future generations.

These sentiments were echoed by the next ecumenical council, held in Ephesus in 431, which forbade any addition to or modification of the Nicene Creed. This implied that this creed, as it then stood, was a sufficiently comprehensive statement of Christian belief.

Constantine promulgated the decrees of the Council of Nicaea as civil laws, and he made the propagation of Arian teachings a criminal offense. His insistence on the use of the word "consubstantial," however, made it more difficult rather than easier to achieve reconciliation, because it forced Christians to choose one faction rather than another. For three hundred years after Nicaea, the church was wracked by Christological disputes far more bitter and more destructive than the original controversy had been.

The Latin-speaking church met with similar results several centuries later, when it insisted upon inserting the phrase "and from the Son" into the Nicene Creed, thereby provoking an estrangement with the Greek-speaking (Orthodox) church which persists to this day.

Nicaea was the first of many occasions on which the attempt to impose upon all Christians a theological formula derived from the conclusion of a metaphysical argument led to the creation or reinforcement of permanent divisions in the church. This was a particularly tragic development, because all theological formulas, by their very nature, attempt to fit God into human

William A. Herr

ways of understanding; and to this extent they necessarily distort and misrepresent the reality which they attempt to convey.

To use human concepts to speak about God always results in some degree of falsification. To use human concepts to draw conclusions about God is presumptuous at best. To use human concepts to try to deduce what God can and cannot do, and what God must and must not do, is self-contradictory and close to blasphemous.

It is one thing to appeal to logical necessity in philosophy, but quite another to try to impose it on God. This not only implicitly denies divine omnipotence, it also contradicts the notion of grace.

This is more or less what Augustine did when he taught that unbaptized babies *must* be damned, as though his own thought processes imposed an obligation on the almighty godhead.

It is what some scholastics did when they constructed the elaborate *quid pro quo* bartering system between humans and God which the Protestant reformers attacked so vehemently.

It is what generations of moral theologians did when they insisted that God must be "just"—that is, that he must conform his behavior to a human way of thinking —as though they never had heard of the parable of the laborers in the vineyard or that of the prodigal son; as though they were offended by the possibility that God might be excessively, "unjustly," generous or merciful.

It is what all the pastors and teachers who presumed to define for their fellow Christians how things appear "in God's eyes" were doing, in ignorance or disregard of St. Paul's warning in *Romans*: "How unsearchable (God's) judgments, how untractable his ways! Who knows the mind of the Lord?"

Theologians had begun by discoursing about God, but as time went on some of them began to create a god of their own—a god who possessed and who necessarily acted in conformity with the attributes which they considered it appropriate for him to possess.

CHAPTER FIVE

Leaving Room for Belief

IT IS possible to discourse about God in a great variety of ways. Even adherents of the same religious faith, if they proceed from different presuppositions, may create radically different means of expressing that faith.

Byzantine theology, for example, places great emphasis upon the distinction between the physical and the spiritual, and between the natural and the supernatural. It does not attempt to apply metaphysical principles to supernature, and it does not presume to impose logical necessity upon God. It looks at spiritual reality as something to be contemplated, not something to be explained. It is more speculative and mystical than analytic.

This tradition has not attached much importance to creating precise definitions of revealed truth, and as a consequence it contains very few dogmas. It is not systematic, and the concept of a *summa theologica* is foreign to it. Byzantine theology, in the exquisitely understated words of the *Catholic Encyclopedia,* "leaves much room for belief."

The theological tradition of the Latin church, on the other hand, long ago accepted the idea that reason can discover the very laws of being, and that these laws apply to both material and spiritual reality. It has presupposed that supernature follows its own intrinsic and unchanging laws, just as nature does, and that the human mind can discover these laws. This means that systematic, scientific knowledge of God is possible; and Latin theology generally has concerned itself with seeking and accumulating this knowledge.

Since scientific knowledge can be given precise definition, this approach tends to encourage dogmatism and provides comparatively little opportunity for individual interpretation. It leaves less "room for belief."

The Latin and Byzantine traditions evolved as they did because they are based upon two different intellectual systems, both of which were developed long before Jesus was born.

Even before the time of Plato, Greek philosophers had established a distinction between two different ways of knowing. "Knowledge" in the strict sense, or the kind of absolutely certain and unchanging understanding which geometry provides, was distinguished from "opinion," or judgments which might be true at one time or in one set of circumstances but false in others.

Geometry achieves absolute certainty by starting with statements which are true by definition and deducing the logical implications of those statements. From the mere definition of a geometric line and a geometric circle, for example, it is possible to reason to conclusions which were true in Euclid's day and never will be disproved.

This kind of information not only is true, it is always and necessarily true. It is applicable only by analogy to our everyday world, however, because there are no objects of experience which exactly fit the definitions of geometric figures. In this sense a geometric circle, which no one has ever seen, is more real than physical things like buttons and coins. It is like their model or ideal, and they can properly be called circles only to the extent to which they resemble it. It is, in fact, precisely this resemblance to a geometric circle which "makes" physical objects more or less round.

It is impossible for anything physical to be perfectly round, because it is impossible to make, or to find, any material object with all of the points on its surface equidistant from its center. Materiality itself, in other words, necessarily implies imperfection, which means that the physical is intrinsically inferior to the spiritual.

IN SEARCH OF CHRISTIAN WISDOM

Plato reasoned that a similar relationship must exist between each group of things which we call by the same name and some kind of perfect model which they resemble, and that it is precisely this resemblance which makes them a particular kind of thing.

There must be something, for example, which makes all brave people brave. Everyone who is brave must share in it to some degree or other, whatever this something is, but no individual can possess all of it. Similarly, something must make all beautiful things beautiful and all good things good.

Seen from this perspective, each physical object is like an imperfect imitation of a perfect and eternal exemplar, or Form. These Forms are more real than the objects of our experience in more or less the same sense that geometric figures are. By the same token, the existence of particular Forms is inexplicable unless one assumes the existence of a single highest Form to which they themselves owe their individual perfections.

This line of reasoning leads directly to the conclusion that there are two different levels of existence. One is imperfect, material, changing, and transitory; the other is perfect, immaterial, unchanging, and eternal. The physical objects which we encounter through sensation, therefore, are like shadows or reflections of immaterial Forms.

William A. Herr

Since reality in the fullest sense is spiritual in nature, true knowledge cannot be attained through sensation but only through the reasoning power of a person's spiritual soul. In theory, one could use information obtained from an analysis of the Forms to create a metaphysical system capable of explaining absolutely everything—a body of knowledge as certain as geometry is, which, once constituted, would be valid for all time because it would be rooted in the very nature of things.

In practice, however, Plato insisted that we can never reach the final and complete answer to anything in this life. So long as our spiritual souls are trapped inside physical bodies, our reliance upon sensation keeps us from apprehending the Forms as they really are. Now we can know them only in a confused and indistinct manner; but after we die we will experience them directly and, as it were, "face to face."

Platonism, therefore, really was not a set of facts or conclusions. It did not claim to bestow understanding, but only to provide an intellectual structure within which each individual could strive toward it. In this sense, Platonism was a quest for an unreachable ideal and an unattainable absolute. It was not so much an attempt to explain individual things as a means of preparing people to search for a single explanation of everything.

IN SEARCH OF CHRISTIAN WISDOM

Through a series of exercises in dialectical reasoning, the student of Platonism gradually was led to an acceptance of the fact that true reality is spiritual and that material substance is illusory, and he or she also was induced to turn away from bodily pleasures and toward those of the spirit. This process resembled in some respects a religious conversion.

Many of the quasi-mystical concepts inherent in Platonism were expanded upon by Plotinus, who wrote more than five and a half centuries after Plato's death.

Plotinus postulated several different levels of reality, from God to formless matter, each of the lower levels emanating from the one above it, and every level containing, in its own unique manner, everything which exists.

He taught that the human soul can ascend, through a process of gradual detachment from material concerns and the practice of contemplation, to an intuitive knowledge of and a direct union with God: an ecstasy of love in which the soul feels itself mystically united with the divine Intellect in which all things have their origin. It is possible, in other words, to experience God directly, although this experience cannot be complete until the soul is totally separated from the body.

At the same time, Plotinus also insisted that since God is absolutely transcendent, it follows that he must be beyond all thought and all comprehension. Because God is one, without parts or divisions or internal distinctions of any kind, it is improper to speak of divine attributes. We may not say that God either possesses or lacks any quality, for to do so would be to imply a limitation of the unlimited. God is to be experienced, not thought or spoken about.

The teachings of Plato and Plotinus were generally accepted by intellectually-minded people in the first centuries of the Christian era.

Not all of the consequences of this acceptance were beneficial. The Platonic view of the human person as a spiritual soul imprisoned inside an animal body whose innate tendencies are opposite to its own, and the notion that matter is of virtually no importance compared to spirit, had the effect of introducing into Christianity an exaggerated other-worldliness and a sometimes pathological aversion to the human body and its natural functions.

This mentality led some Christians to deny the reality of Christ's incarnation. It encouraged others to engage in excessively rigorous and sometimes self-destructive ascetic practices. It also tended to foster a belief that the infliction of any degree of physical harm, even including death, might be justified if it helped to "save" a person's soul—as though it were souls that Jesus had come to save, rather than people.

Platonic and neoplatonic philosophy, however, also provided early Christian writers with many of the concepts which they used to express and defend their most fundamental religious beliefs, and to create doctrinal formulas which have been accepted as standards of orthodoxy from their day to our own.

Plato's teaching that the human soul is immortal, for example, and that it naturally longs to escape from this world and return to God, was looked upon as a philosophical argument for the afterlife. The belief that there is a single supreme spiritual reality, unchanging and eternal, and that everything else in the universe owes its existence to this supreme reality, provided a ready-made metaphysical justification for the concepts of monotheism and creation. Plotinus's insistence that evil is merely the absence of good was utilized by Christian apologists to refute Manicheanism.

Neoplatonism, particularly as transmitted through the works of Greek-speaking writers, had a profound influence upon the development of Christian mystical theology, especially that approach to mysticism sometimes referred to as the *via negativa*. Origen, the most influential of the early Christian theologians, was fol-

William A. Herr

lowing a neoplatonic tradition when he insisted that it is more proper to apply to God negative concepts such as "immaterial" and "unlimited" than positive concepts like "spiritual" or "omnipotent."

Basil of Caesarea, Ambrose, and Gregory of Nyssa, among many others, made extensive use of Platonic and neoplatonic sources. Augustine underwent a radical spiritual transformation while reading what he called "certain Platonic books," books which probably had been written by Plotinus; and he went so far as to identify the three divine persons of the Christian trinity with the three Plotinian "hypostases," or first principles.

As late as 1259, in *The Mind's Journey to God,* St. Bonaventure outlined an approach to Christian mysticism based on concepts—including that of a hierarchy of levels of reality—which can be traced directly back to Plotinus.

The objects of our everyday experience, Bonaventure wrote, are filled with *vestigia Dei* (literally, "footprints of God"), or an overwhelming multitude of examples of God's handiwork, each testifying in some manner to one or more of the creator's perfections. Through observation and contemplation of these *vestigia,* it is possible, with the assistance of grace, to attain a direct mystical vision of God.

IN SEARCH OF CHRISTIAN WISDOM

This means that we are surrounded by objects which symbolize something greater than themselves. The entire physical world, according to Bonaventure, is "a ladder for ascending to God." Here again, as in Plato, the value of a material thing lies not in itself but in the higher reality which it reflects.

Bonaventure valued knowledge derived from direct experience far more than that based on reasoning, and he urged every Christian to try to experience God as fully as possible through contemplation, even though only a few may be able to reach the highest levels of mystical rapture.

The content of mystical encounters, however, is intensely personal, and difficult if not impossible to communicate to others. The reality is acknowledged as true because it has been directly experienced, not because it can be proved or explained or even understood—let alone subjected to logical analysis. The prudent person does not attempt to describe the ineffable: he or she merely testifies to its existence and points in the direction where it may be found.

This manner of approaching God was entirely consistent with the Byzantine tradition as it existed at that time and as it still exists today. It was an approach, however, which was destined to fall out of favor in the West.

William A. Herr

In the same year that *The Mind's Journey to God* was written, Thomas Aquinas was appointed theological advisor to the papal curia, after having taught theology in Paris for seven years. And the theology which Aquinas had been teaching, and which eventually would become the dominant tradition in the Latin-speaking church, was based upon a very different philosophical orientation.

CHAPTER SIX

With Relentless Logic

PLATO and Aristotle both tried to find a way to make absolutely certain statements about the objects of our sense experience.

Plato hypothesized that the various characteristics of these objects must be caused in some way by eternal and unchanging Forms. Since he was unable to explain how we can come to a knowledge of these Forms starting from sensation, he was forced to assume that we must have encountered them in a previous existence. He concluded that it is these Forms which are the foundation of all true knowledge and that, to all intents and purposes, the objects of sensation cannot be known at all.

Aristotle approached the problem in a different way; and some of the conclusions which this approach made it possible for him to draw were destined, more than a thousand years after his death, to change the basic orientation of Roman Catholic theology.

Aristotle sought to identify the explanatory principles

of individual things—the reasons why things are the way they are—including the explanatory principles of reasoning itself. This led him to undertake the first systematic analysis of the reasoning process.

Analysis involves reducing something to its constituent parts, and Aristotle reduced reasoning to propositions and propositions to terms. He believed that there are certain syllogisms, or ways of combining propositions, which relate their terms to one another in such a way that a true conclusion always will follow from true premises.

So long as one utilizes the proper types of syllogisms, therefore, one can reason step by inexorable step toward what must be true; and the reason why each conclusion must be true is precisely the structure of the reasoning which led to it. In this way we can draw conclusions about things which we have never experienced, and know for a certainty that what we have concluded is true.

At the same time, although he shared Plato's desire to find a way to make true and certain statements about the ever-changing objects of sensation, Aristotle, unlike Plato, believed that change is part of the reality which must be explained. He tried to build the foundation for a true science of sensible things upon an analysis of what change actually involves.

IN SEARCH OF CHRISTIAN WISDOM

Aristotle felt justified in taking it for granted that change does not mean that an entire object suddenly goes out of existence and another object simultaneously takes its place. It means, rather, that one or more of the qualities of a thing are replaced by other qualities, while an underlying substratum remains the same.

A round piece of clay, for example, can become flat; and a flat piece can become round. This means that each piece of clay is a composite: its shape and color and texture all are different from the material, the "clayness," which remains the same while its various attributes change. The same thing is true of every other physical thing.

Another type of change involves the transformation of one kind of thing into another kind, as when the human body turns fruit and vegetables into flesh and bone and blood. This proves that matter itself must be a composite. There must be a kind of indeterminate matter and also something which determines whether a particular portion of this matter, at a particular moment in time, will be an ear of corn or a human blood cell.

Aristotle believed that there must be immaterial principles of some kind, or "forms," which cause these determinations. When a caterpillar is transformed into a butterfly, what really happens is that a certain piece of matter loses one form and acquires another. In effect, he held that the constantly changing world of sensation and the static, eternal world of Plato's Forms both are present in the same objects.

These conclusions, and many others like them, Aristotle considered to be applicable to all material objects, even those which no one has yet experienced, because they are based upon an analysis of the very nature of material things. Similar analysis can be made of the nature of spiritual things.

Aristotelian metaphysics, in short, can be looked upon as a mechanism for reducing any existing thing to a limited number of explanatory principles. Once all of these principles had been identified, one could logically deduce how any given thing must behave in any specific circumstances. Although Aristotle himself continually stressed the importance of empirical observation, he created an instrument which was perfectly suited to the drawing of *a priori* conclusions.

This instrument made possible what Plato had been unable to accomplish: it provided the foundation for a metaphysics which can explain absolutely everything, provided that one accepts its presuppositions. It was possible, for example, for Aristotle not only to conclude that the concentric spheres into which the heavenly regions were thought to be divided must be moved by spirits, but also to deduce the precise mechanism which must be used to produce this motion—something which no one could possibly observe.

Aristotle's logical concepts were introduced into Christian Europe through the translations and commentaries of Boethius; and by the beginning of the eleventh century, theologians such as Berengarius of Tours were using them to draw conclusions about what must be true and not true about God and the sacraments.

Before long it became apparent that the systematic application of logic to religious beliefs was beginning to change the way in which theological inquiry was being conducted. St. Peter Damian, who died in 1072, protested that reason was threatening to dominate theology, rather than merely being its handmaid.

This was happening in part because Aristotelian logic was such a powerful tool for drawing true conclusions from true premises and for distinguishing valid from invalid reasonings that it tended to make those who were expert in its use assume that what is logical must be true and what is illogical must be false. This posed serious problems for people who maintained that God is literally omnipotent and who really believed that his ways are beyond our comprehension.

Peter Damian, for example, was so anxious to establish the fact that the Almighty is not restricted by the norms of human reasoning that he insisted that God can change the past, bringing it about that something which already has occurred should not have occurred. Similar arguments about the relation between logical necessity and divine omnipotence were destined to continue for hundreds of years.

Another reason why the rediscovery of Aristotelian logic had such a profound effect upon theology was that this logic was designed to analyze simple, unequivocal declarative sentences arranged in syllogistic form. It was next to useless in dealing with allegories or poetical expressions or figures of speech of any kind.

Logically-minded theologians therefore tended to concentrate upon those problems and arguments which could be expressed in syllogisms. As a result, they turned their attention more to the writings of other theologians and correspondingly less to Scripture—which, like most other religious writing, does not lend itself to this kind of analysis. Otloh of St. Emmeran, a contemporary of Damian, complained that some theologians of his day seemed to think more highly of Boethius than of the Bible—but not even he could have imagined how prophetic his words would become.

Less than one hundred years after Otloh's death, Peter Lombard finished work on a book of citations from the writings of various theologians, along with his own analysis and conclusions. In 1222 Alexander of Halles broke with a centuries-old tradition by using this *Book of Sentences* rather than the Bible as the basis for his lectures, and other professors quickly followed suit.

Before long, all candidates for a degree in theology were required to write a commentary on Peter's *Sentences*. Analyzing the teachings of other theologians was indeed becoming more important than studying Scripture, just as Otloh had feared.

This tendency was greatly reinforced when Aristotle's metaphysical writings were introduced into Western Europe, starting in the latter half of the twelfth century. It was not long before professors at the University of Paris, which then was the leading center of theological scholarship in the West, began to accept the idea that Aristotle had discovered the explanatory principles of being itself, and thus that it was valid to apply his metaphysical concepts to everything which exists. This allowed them to create an enormous number of new issues about which they could dispute with one another.

Are angels, for example, composed of matter as well as form? If they are, then this angelic matter must be incorporeal—but is there really such a thing as incorporeal matter, and if so what are its properties? If, on the other hand, angels are forms without matter, then one angel could not be distinguished from another unless

William A. Herr

their forms were different. According to Aristotelian principles, however, different forms constitute different species, which means that each angel must be a species unto itself—a conclusion which many people found preposterous.

The possibilities for speculation were almost endless. If one can subject angels to metaphysical analysis, why could the same analysis not be applied to the doctrine of the Incarnation and to the other great Christian mysteries, or even to the Trinity and to the nature of God himself?

Those who followed this line of reasoning naturally tended to respond to religious questions with metaphysical answers rather than with scriptural ones. It did not seem unreasonable, after all, to place more confidence in logical arguments based upon Aristotle's description of the innermost nature of things than in anyone's personal opinion, even one's own, about how a particular biblical passage should be interpreted.

This is more or less what Thomas Aquinas did. He assumed—and it had to be an assumption, because there can be no decisive rational proof of the matter one way or another—that the same metaphysical principles which Aristotle had used to explain the natural world can be applied to all of supernatural reality and in particular to God, who is potentially the most knowable of all beings.

Aquinas then proceeded, in a systematic and almost relentless fashion, to draw out the logical implications of that assumption.

He insisted, for example, in opposition to St. Bonaventure, that angels are pure spirits, forms without matter, and that each individual angel is a distinct species. He believed that the Aristotelian principles which supported this conclusion carried more weight than the fact that Scripture describes some angels as performing similar functions and therefore, by implication, as belonging to the same species.

Aquinas argued that everything which exists, even a supernatural being, is what it is and acts as it does because of its own intrinsic nature. Even God must act in conformity with the kind of being which he is—which implies that, if we knew enough about the divine nature, we could predict what he will and will not do.

Bonaventure, on the other hand, willingly conceded Aristotle's preeminence as a naturalist but considered his metaphysics to be flawed from a Christian perspective because it does not and cannot take account of truths which can be known only by faith. In particular, he believed that Aristotelian metaphysical principles cannot validly be applied to any supernatural reality and least of all to God.

Aquinas also opposed Bonaventure, and rejected what had been the prevailing Christian tradition since at least the time of Augustine, by agreeing with Aristotle that knowing, rather than loving, is the highest and most noble human activity. He emphasized, for example, the ways in which we can proceed from the objects of our daily experience to an intellectual knowledge of God, whereas Bonaventure concentrated upon showing how these same objects can help us to ascend to a personal love-relationship with him. Even our eternal reward was intellectual in nature for Aquinas, rather than affective as for Bonaventure.

(It is unfortunate that so little is known about the spiritual experience which Aquinas underwent near the end of his life, following which he is reported to have said that everything which he had written seemed worthless to him, and after which he never wrote again. Perhaps, in the end, he discovered that Bonaventure had been right after all.)

This shift in emphasis from the heart to the head became more and more deeply ingrained in Roman Catholicism as Thomism gained a position of preeminence over the older theological traditions.

One of the first steps in this process occurred when

IN SEARCH OF CHRISTIAN WISDOM

Aquinas's *Summa Theologica* replaced the *Sentences* of Peter Lombard as the basis for lectures in university theology departments. Substituting the *Sentences* for the Bible had meant enhancing the status of the Fathers of the Church at the expense of the status of Scripture; substituting the *Summa* for the *Sentences* meant enhancing the status of a single theologian at the expense of the status of the Fathers. This had some unfortunate consequences.

The very comprehensiveness and logical consistency of Aquinas's system, and the fact that it was based upon principles supposedly grounded in an analysis of being, helped to create the impression in some people's minds that Christianity could and should be passed on to posterity by formulating and transmitting objective facts about God, rather than by teaching people how they might draw closer to him. Catholic theology, in other words, became more speculative and less pastoral.

Theology carried on in this manner, however, tends to encourage people to look upon faith as knowledge rather than as commitment. It therefore runs the risk of becoming a substitute for God.

CHAPTER SEVEN

Erecting the Great Wall

THE tendency of many scholastic theologians—
especially followers of Duns Scotus and Thomas
Aquinas—to base their teachings upon the logical implications of metaphysical speculation rather than upon
scripture and the writings of the early church Fathers
did not go unchallenged.

Among the most vociferous opponents of the theories
which these writers were expounding was William of
Ockham, a younger contemporary of Scotus. Ockham,
like Peter Damian three hundred years earlier, insisted
that any school of thought which refused to acknowledge God's total and absolute omnipotence must be er-
roneous, and that Aristotelian philosophy and any
theological system based upon it did precisely that.

Everything in the universe, Ockham believed, is absolutely contingent upon the divine will from each in-
stant to the next and there is no way to predict with
certainty what that will might be. God need not act rea-
sonably, or fairly, or even consistently; and he can at

74

any time cause any event to follow any other event. This means that there can be no intrinsic relationship between what we call causes and effects, which in turn means that one of the basic principles upon which scholastic theology rests is invalid.

God, for example, might choose to reward a particular action one day and punish it the next. No one can be confident, if he or she does something, that God will respond in one way rather than in another—or even that he will respond at all. It is therefore impossible to "earn" any supernatural merit whatsoever, let alone salvation. It also is impossible to use metaphysical arguments to draw valid conclusions about God. We can learn, from experience or from revelation, what God has done in the past but we are not able to reason to a knowledge of what he must do or even what he will do in the future.

Ockham's basic criticism of the scholastics was that, by relying too heavily upon Aristotle and the power of the human intellect, they had arrived at false conclusions. About a century and a half later, Erasmus, the most famous and respected scholar of his day, leveled some far more serious accusations: that scholasticism had usurped the authority formerly accorded to scripture, that it was turning Christian belief into a mere compendium of mechanical formulas, and that it was responsible for channeling too much of the church's energy and resources into academic theorizing and too little into the cultivation of Christian virtues.

In 1517 he wrote to Albrecht of Brandenburg that "Formerly he was a heretic who dissented from the gospels, the articles of faith, or something of comparable authority. Now, if anyone disagrees in any way with Thomas, or even if anyone disagrees with a false theory which some sophist in the schools recently invented, he is called a heretic."

In a letter to his friend Paul Volz, he complained that scholastic theologians "examine minutely each single topic and so define each as if they mistrusted . . . the goodness of Christ, while they set forth precisely how he ought to reward or punish each deed. . . ."

Others expressed similar beliefs. Jean Colet, one of the leading figures of the English Renaissance, was convinced, according to Erasmus, that Thomas Aquinas had "tainted the whole doctrine of Christ with his profane philosophy."

Whereas a number of modern writers have argued about whether or not the "Christian philosophy of the middle ages" really was philosophy, men such as Ockham, Erasmus, and Colet had grave doubts as to whether the scholastic theology of the middle ages really was Christian.

IN SEARCH OF CHRISTIAN WISDOM

In the end, however, these viewpoints did not prevail. As the Protestant movement began to gain ground, and defections from the Roman church increased, those aspects of Catholic intellectual life which Erasmus had found most objectionable became more and more firmly entrenched.

Catholicism grew less tolerant of divergent opinions and of the unsupervised investigation of religious matters, particularly by lay people. It became increasingly authoritarian, and left less and less "room for belief." It looked upon its theology even more than previously as a treasury of received knowledge, whose safekeeping was entrusted to a group of highly trained experts, rather than as a never-ending process of creative inquiry based upon personal religious experience.

"Is it not possible," Erasmus had asked, "to have fellowship with the Father, Son and Holy Spirit, without being able to explain philosophically the distinction between them, and between the nativity of the Son and the procession of the Holy Spirit? . . . All that is of faith should be condensed into a very few articles, and the same should be done for all that concerns the Christian way of life." There cannot be peace and harmony in the Christian community, he had insisted, "unless we define as little as possible."

In the chaotic years of the Counter-Reformation,

William A. Herr

however, Catholicism's first priority was to distinguish its teaching from that of Protestantism as clearly and precisely as possible. It erected a solid wall of dogmas and definitions between the two, and it undertook to defend every inch of that wall against all enemies both outside and inside the church.

The perfect instrument for these purposes lay close at hand. If one's primary concern is to draw distinctions, formulate definitions, and refute objections, one could not wish for a more powerful intellectual tool than scholasticism, the product of centuries of disputations in university lecture halls on thousands of different topics. Scholastic theology spoke with authority and confidence, which was precisely the tone with which Catholicism felt it necessary to express itself.

The fact that many of the Protestant polemicists had demonstrated a particular aversion to scholastic theology, of course, did nothing to diminish its value in the eyes of the counter-reformers.

Under these circumstances, scholasticism became more than a means of analyzing disputed issues: it became a disputed issue itself, separate from the faith which it was supposed to be expressing. In some cases the primary point of contention between Protestant and Catholic theologians was not the fundamental truth of a particular religious doctrine, but simply whether or not that belief should be formulated in scholastic terms.

Such a situation arose in 1541, when leading Catholic and Lutheran theologians met in the German city of Regensburg in an attempt to resolve the major doctrinal issues separating them.

All parties at this conference agreed that the body and blood of Christ both are truly and physically present in the Eucharistic bread and wine. The Lutherans, however, refused to accept the scholastic term "transubstantiation," with its Aristotelian overtones. They proposed instead a formula which affirmed the fact of Christ's presence without formulating a metaphysical explanation of that fact. This proposal was totally in harmony with the spirit of Erasmus, but ultimately it was rejected.

Four years after this ill-fated meeting, the Council of Trent began turning scholastic concepts such as transubstantiation into articles of faith, thereby making reconciliation between European Christians even more difficult.

It is unquestionably true that the church has a duty to ensure that the teachings of Jesus are faithfully and accurately transmitted from generation to generation. It also is true, however, that the primary reason for striving to maintain doctrinal purity is to unite the faithful, not to divide them, and that the creation of dogmatic definitions often has precisely the opposite effect.

So powerful was the urge to distinguish and separate and condemn in the years following Trent, in fact, that where there were no Protestants to combat, Catholics sometimes turned against one another. Thus the Dominicans and the Jesuits carried on a vicious polemical struggle against each other for twenty-five years, simply because they disagreed about how to reconcile belief in free will with belief that a grace which cannot be merited is both necessary and sufficient for salvation.

What made this disedifying spectacle all the more senseless is the fact that the issue over which the participants were so enthusiastically battling with their brothers in Christ—like many other theological conundrums—probably has no rational solution. There are many questions about the details of God's providence concerning which, in the words of Erasmus, "everyone should be left to follow his own judgment, because there is a great obscurity in these matters."

This suggests that, of all those who engage in theoretical speculation, theologians should be the most humble, and the most tolerant, and the most reluctant to condemn the opinions of others. It should go without saying, given Christ's explicit commandment that his followers should love one another, that this should be particularly true of Christian theologians. This obviously has not always been the case.

It may be objected that a great deal has changed in the last twenty-five years, and that newer theologies—based upon Heidegger or Marx or the existentialists or some other fashionable philosophical movement—have replaced Thomism in the curricula of Catholic institutions.

One reply to this objection is that, in spite of these changes, many vestiges of the old ways of thinking still remain. Consider this statement from the entry on "Eucharist" in *The Catholic Encyclopedia*, hardly a reactionary publication: "In other words, God obliges himself to give the graces of Redemption in a manner befitting the state and condition of each one implicated in the offering of the Mass."

Ignoring for the moment the infelicitous choice of the word "implicated," consider the phrase "God obliges himself." What could this expression possibly mean? Even if one were to admit that it might mean something, how could anyone conceivably know whether it is true or not? Indeed, no less an authority than Jesus himself seemed convinced that God is not aware of being under any such obligation.

Such a statement, in all likelihood, is the product of

William A. Herr

someone's having concluded, hundreds of years ago, that it would be unjust of God to bestow his graces upon his children without regard for their merits, and therefore that he somehow is "obliged" not to do so. Surely St. Paul's admonition bears repeating once again: "Who knows the mind of God?"

The more crucial issue, however, is not what type of theology is most appropriate to express the various truths of Christianity, but rather what the relationship between theology and other forms of God-centered activity should be.

The problem, once again, is not with theology itself, but rather with a mentality which places more value on attempts to explain God than on attempts to encounter him. This is not something which can be corrected by substituting Karl Rahner or Hans Kung for Aquinas. It has to do with the nature of the theological enterprise itself.

Theology we will always have with us, because it helps to satisfy our innate human desire to understand. There are other human desires, however, non-intellectual ones, which are equally or even more compelling and which no theology ever will be able to satisfy. The human spirit hungers for the satisfaction of its own particular needs, just as the human intellect does; and that spirit does not live by explanations alone.

IN SEARCH OF CHRISTIAN WISDOM

It is certain that people of our own day have the same spiritual natures and the same fundamental spiritual needs as did the people to whom Jesus preached. It is far from certain, however, what people of our day need to do in order to experience that sense of spiritual fulfillment which Jesus provided. Even more challenging is the question of whether or not there is a way for Christians to achieve both spiritual and intellectual satisfaction.

Is there another means of approaching God besides studying abstract theories on one hand and abandoning oneself to unquestioning fundamentalism on the other —some middle ground between academic theology and television evangelism?

Is it possible to establish a rational framework which could help to guide both the mind and the heart step by step to God, while allowing—or even requiring—each individual to undertake that journey himself or herself? If so, what kind of framework would accomplish this, and what benefits could it provide?

We have seen how attempts were made to utilize first Platonism and then Aristotelianism, two systems whose purpose was to discover and transmit factual information, to explain the Christian faith and we have seen how these attempts influenced the evolution of Christianity in general and of Catholicism in particular.

William A. Herr

There are other types of systems, however, which might be used to help people actually draw closer to God: systems whose purpose is to elicit from the listener or disciple an inner response and a personal commitment. One such system was utilized by a man who had a great deal in common with Jesus, even though he lived long before the beginning of the Christian era.

CHAPTER EIGHT

The Socratic Path

B EFORE Socrates began his life's work, which was sometime in the latter half of the fifth century B.C., the learned men of Greece had spent most of their time either studying mathematics or trying to understand the physical universe: what it is made of, what its unifying principles are, and how to explain phenomena such as motion and change and time.

Thales, for example, believed that everything is made out of water. Others taught that the primary stuff of the universe is air, or fire, or "the unlimited." Heraclitus said that everything is constantly changing; Parmenides said that nothing ever changes.

Socrates, however, was not interested in mathematics, or change, or the composition of the universe. He was interested in how people live—which is why Cicero wrote that Socrates had "brought philosophy from the heavens down to earth." More specifically, Socrates was interested in wisdom.

William A. Herr

Wisdom is something quite different from information. Wisdom has to do not with how much a person knows, but with what he or she does. Those who impress us as being wise are not necessarily the most intelligent or the best educated, but those who exercise good judgment.

These people weigh matters carefully and are not misled by appearances or by the opinions of others. They are able to see everything in its proper perspective, and they put first things first. Wise people know why they are doing what they do. They seem to be in control of their lives.

What makes it possible to gain control of one's life is the fact that every life is made up of choices and every choice, even if we do not realize it at the time, presupposes values. How we live depends upon what we choose, and what we choose depends upon the value which we place on different things. In a very real sense, what we value determines who we are.

Values are simply another way of saying that one thing is more important, more "valuable," than something else. All of us have values, whether or not we take the trouble to find out what they are. Someone who had no values could not make choices, which means that such a person could not live.

Our values, however, may not be consistent or well

thought out and they may not correspond to the reality of things. We may place more value upon one thing than it deserves, and less upon another. We may place great value on something one day, and very little on it the next. We may place equal value on things which are mutually incompatible.

We may habitually act on impulses, valuing whatever seems attractive at the moment, so that there is no purposefulness or consistency in what we do. In this case our lives will be no more than what Aristotle called "a succession of unrelated emotional experiences."

Wisdom enables us to make sound judgments about values, to guide our lives by values which do not conflict with one another, and therefore to live in a coherent manner. Wisdom helps us to ensure that what we do in the short run will be in harmony with what we want in the long run.

Wisdom also makes it possible to prioritize values: to establish a kind of hierarchy, so that lower values do not interfere with higher ones. It helps us to arrange things so that, to use Andrew Greeley's expression, the important does not interfere with the essential.

Any coherent system of values must be founded on one supreme value, something to which everything else must be subordinated—money, perhaps, or pleasure, or power, or fame. The task to which Socrates devoted

William A. Herr

himself was to champion the cause of wisdom: to convince his fellow Athenians that wisdom is more important than any other earthly possession, and to assist them in acquiring it.

This is a somewhat abridged version of how Socrates himself described this mission when he was on trial for his life:

> As long as I draw breath, and have my faculties . . . I shall go on saying, in my usual way, "My very good friend . . . Are you not ashamed that you give your attention to acquiring as much money as possible, and similarly with reputation and honor, and give no attention or thought to truth, and understanding, and the perfection of your soul . . .?
>
> I shall do this to everyone that I meet, young or old, foreigner or fellow-citizen; but especially to you my fellow-citizens, inasmuch as you are closer to me in kinship. This, I do assure you, is what my God commands . . . for I spend all my time going about trying to persuade you, young and old, to make your first and chief concern not for your bodies nor for your possessions, but for the highest welfare of your souls, proclaiming as I go, "Wealth does not bring goodness, but goodness brings wealth and every other blessing, both to the individual and to the State."

IN SEARCH OF CHRISTIAN WISDOM

There is nothing particularly remarkable about these words. Many people throughout history have made similar statements, but Socrates differed from most of the others in two important respects.

First, like Jesus, he concentrated upon transforming the lives of individual people one by one, rather than attempting to enact better laws or drawing up blueprints for a more just society.

In addition Socrates—again, like Jesus—never wrote anything. He did not elaborate a philosophical system, and he gave no lectures. Socrates taught by personal example and by asking questions. He did not try to put something new into people's heads, but to draw out something which already was there. What he had to offer was not a message but a method: a method to help people to discover and clarify the implications of things which they already knew but did not realize that they knew.

Socrates adopted this approach because he understood, nearly twenty-five hundred years ago, something which many people still refuse to admit: that wisdom and morality cannot be transmitted from one person to another in the same way that something like arithmetic can be.

Wisdom is not a science. It is a way of life, and it must be rediscovered—perhaps even reinvented—by each person who desires to acquire it. One gains wisdom not merely by receiving a certain set of values but by accepting them, thinking them through, making them one's own, committing oneself to them: in short, by choosing them.

The fact that Socrates taught by asking questions does not mean that he was indifferent to the choices which his students made. He believed that, if he questioned them skillfully enough, he could bring them to a recognition and acceptance of objective reality, of those things which really are good and which really are true. This belief rested upon a conviction that denying reality sooner or later will lead one to contradict oneself.

Since adherence to a particular set of values is a matter of choice rather than of proof, Socrates really was trying to encourage people to make a leap of faith. This kind of commitment, as we have said before, cannot be put into people; it must be drawn out of them. Socrates believed that the function of a true teacher is to cultivate and develop what already is present in an indistinct and incomplete form within the student. This is why he compared his role to that of a midwife.

Socrates often insisted that he himself did not know anything—by which he meant, I believe, that what really was important was not what he himself had discovered but what his method could help other people to discover for themselves. By the same token, what is important for our purposes is not so much the specific things which Socrates was trying to teach, but the method which he was using to teach them.

The idea of a teacher who is not interested in transmitting knowledge may seem strange to us, but it is quite familiar to other cultures. In *The Spirit Master* John Shea tells a Zen story which illustrates this.

"What does your master teach?" asked a visitor.
"Nothing," said the disciple.
"Then why does he give discourses?"
"He only points the way—he teaches nothing."
The visitor couldn't make sense out of this, so the disciple made it clearer: "If the Master were to teach, we would make beliefs out of his teachings. The Master is not concerned with what we believe—only with what we see."

Not everyone agreed with what Socrates was trying to do. While he was exhorting the citizens of Athens to attend to the perfection of their souls, a group of men known to history as "Sophists" were disseminating a very different message.

The Sophists made their living by catering to wealthy families who wanted to make certain that their sons would enjoy successful careers in public life, even if they did not really deserve to succeed. For a fee—and often a very substantial fee—they offered to teach these young men enough logical tricks and rhetorical techniques to enable them to pass themselves off as being wise and virtuous, without having to go to the trouble of actually becoming wise and virtuous.

This kind of offer raised a number of troublesome questions, some of which still are being asked today. What difference does it make, in the final analysis, whether what one says is true or false, so long as people accept it as true? If someone can make others believe that he or she is honest, what extra advantage is there in actually being honest? If one is honored, what does it matter if he or she is not really honorable?

Is not the illusion of possessing any admirable quality just as good as actually possessing it, so long as the illusion can be maintained? Appearances, in other words, may be just as good as reality—and sometimes even better.

This way of thinking threatened to undermine everything which Socrates was trying to accomplish, just as it always has threatened to undermine what Jesus tried to accomplish. Socrates believed most fervently that what really is true is far more important than what merely appears to be true; and for this reason he did everything he could to counteract the influence of the Sophists, particularly their influence upon the young.

Sophism, however, is difficult to argue against, because it is impossible to formulate a logical argument to prove the value of reality. The most that one can do is to show that it is impossible to deny it without contradiction.

Socrates fought against the Sophists, not by using syllogisms to refute them, but in the same way in which he taught his own students: by asking questions and by constructing analogies. It was in this manner that he attempted to demonstrate that Sophism is contradicted by certain basic facts which no one can deny in practice, no matter what he or she might hold in theory.

It is quite possible to teach Sophism—indeed, many people are becoming extremely wealthy by teaching it today—but no one can really live Sophism. Not even a Sophist, for example, would be content with eating only the illusion of food and not the food itself. Clever arguments can win debates, but they cannot change reality; and sooner or later reality always prevails.

The method of Socrates was extremely effective, too effective for his own good. He made his fellow citizens feel so uncomfortable about not paying attention to truth, and understanding, and the perfection of their souls that finally they put him to death. During his lifetime, however, Socrates was able to completely transform the lives of some of the most outstanding people of his age, Plato among them. One might even say that he converted them.

Yes, the method of Socrates is indeed effective, provided that one has the skill and the patience to utilize it. But it means beginning all over again with each individual, because everyone must discover and formulate his or her own answers to the teacher's questions, even if the answers all turn out to be the same in the end. And not all teachers have that much patience.

After the death of Socrates, Plato attempted to find a shortcut by turning what his mentor had looked upon as an art into a science. Rather than personally leading students through a step-by-step examination of the presuppositions which underlay their conscious beliefs, so that they could discover for themselves what is true, he sought to determine once and for all what the truth is and then write it down so that it could be passed on to others. Whereas Socrates had concentrated upon fostering personal commitment, Plato concentrated on gathering and preserving factual knowledge.

Not satisfied with this, he went one step further and set about describing how society could be organized so that the majority of people would never even have to know the truth. He devoted his final book entirely to legislation, apparently in the belief that the best way— or at least the easiest way—to make people good is to make the right laws.

(It is an interesting fact that although Plato wrote more than two dozen dialogues, "The Laws" is the only one in which the character of Socrates does not appear. This may have been a coincidence, but it also is possible that Plato himself realized that the approach which he was advocating in this book was one with which Socrates would have preferred not to be associated.)

Plato was followed by others who shared his ambition of creating a "scientific" body of speculative knowledge, one which would remain true and certain for all time—although each had a different conception of what that knowledge consisted of. And so philosophy, which literally means "the love of wisdom," was transformed into a mere collection of theories, one branch of inquiry alongside many others. The love of wisdom was superseded by the pursuit of knowledge.

Socrates, like Jesus, offered his disciples an invitation; and, like Jesus, he was followed by men who did their best to turn his invitation into a collection of facts and a set of rules.

CHAPTER NINE

Fostering Christian Wisdom

THERE are many different varieties of wisdom. There is a kind of professional wisdom, which helps doctors, lawyers, and businessmen to exercise good judgment in their occupations. There is a wisdom based upon personal experience, which helps parents to become effective and compassionate teachers of their young. There is a philosophic type of wisdom, through which a person is able to lead his or her life according to a well-reasoned and coherent set of beliefs.

There also is a specifically Christian kind of wisdom: a way of living based upon a Christian hierarchy of values.

It was values, after all, which Jesus attempted to teach us. He asked his followers to live in accordance with the same value system which he himself embraced, one in which nothing has any importance except insofar as it brings one closer to God. The Christian subordinates everything else—money, pleasure, power, fame—to this one supreme value.

IN SEARCH OF CHRISTIAN WISDOM

This means that the Christian and the non-Christian live in different worlds. They walk side by side in the same physical world, but they inhabit different value-worlds. Even the events of everyday life—birth, death, joy, suffering, work, marriage, sexuality—have different meanings for them.

This concept of two coexisting value-worlds was given its classic expression by St. Augustine, who believed that the driving force of all human history has been an irreconcilable conflict between those who value God more than anything else and those who do not. Since their value systems are incompatible, these two groups always will stand in opposition to one another.

It is not difficult to find examples of this conflict between Christian and non-Christian values today. We can see it in the best-selling books which assert that the way to become successful is not to love one's neighbors but to manipulate or intimidate them. We can see it whenever public figures proclaim, either explicitly or by implication, that qualities such as honesty, compassion, simplicity, kindness, and faithfulness are not the hallmarks of a mature and responsible person but the distinguishing characteristics of a weakling or a simpleton.

The same kind of conflict between Christian and non-Christian values also can exist within a single individual, if he or she tries to live by two different standards at the same time. This is the situation which Jesus described as trying to serve two masters. A person may be wise as an accountant or architect, or as a parent, or even as a philosopher, and yet be foolish as a Christian.

If we wish to lead Christian lives, we must live according to a Christian conception of which things are more important and which things are less. This is not something which anyone can do consistently, day in and day out, by relying upon factual knowledge. It requires the cultivation of a Christian form of practical wisdom, the kind of wisdom which enables a person to live habitually in the Christian value world.

Christian wisdom, like the philosophic wisdom which Socrates urged his students to pursue, cannot really be taught. Faith cannot be handed down from one person to another, and neither can adherence to a particular set of values. No two people's faith or values are exactly the same, any more than their love is.

Jesus taught us values, just as our fathers and mothers taught us values but this knowledge by itself will not make anyone virtuous. Jesus pointed out a new level of reality in things, but it is up to each individual to make that reality his or her own by living it minute by minute and year after year.

IN SEARCH OF CHRISTIAN WISDOM

Values cannot be acquired by following rules. The most that any list of do's and don'ts can accomplish, no matter who draws it up, is to regulate people's behavior, not to touch their hearts. This may give the appearance of virtue, but it cannot produce the reality—which is not much different from what the Sophists of ancient Athens were attempting to sell.

While it is true that faith cannot be proved by reason, the decision to believe or not to believe, like the decision to love or not to love, is determined in part by the values which one has adopted. Every form of religious faith presupposes certain basic value-related beliefs which reason may indeed be able to prove.

Christian values are not simply a manifestation of Christian faith: they also are a foundation and a preparation for it. The fact that Jesus himself was unable to convert the Rich Young Man—a person who, scripture seems to indicate, very much wanted to be converted—illustrates this. The seed which Jesus sowed could not take root in the young man's heart, because the man placed more value upon his money than upon the treasures of the spirit which Jesus offered to him.

Indeed, it is difficult to see how anyone could possibly choose to accept the invitation to "sell all that you have, and give the money to the poor, and follow me" if he or she believes that wealth is the greatest of all

William A. Herr

goods. It is even difficult to see how a person who has never stopped to prioritize his or her values, who is always too occupied with work or play or the distractions of the moment to engage in serious reflection, could ever make a firm commitment to follow Jesus— or to do anything else.

It was the Rich Young Man's hierarchy of values, or perhaps his lack of such a hierarchy, which kept him from following Jesus; and one cannot help but wonder whether he would have made a different decision if he had spent some time with Socrates first.

The great majority of the followers of Christ, going back perhaps even to apostolic times, have accepted the idea that human reason can make an important contribution to Christianity, although they often have disagreed about what the nature of that contribution should be.

We have seen how reason was employed to construct elaborate theological systems. It also should be possible, however, to develop an intellectual approach to Christianity which takes its inspiration from Socrates rather than from Plato, or Aristotle, or any of the other metaphysical system-builders.

This would be an approach to religion—to the establishing of a personal relationship with God—rather than an approach to a theology or to a doctrine. It would be a framework for asking questions, a technique for achieving insights which point out and suggest but do not give definite answers, not a mechanism for transmitting formalized beliefs. It would be an approach which utilized reason to foster a love of Christian wisdom, just as Socrates used reason to foster a love of philosophical wisdom.

This kind of approach to Christianity could help people to make explicit and examine and prioritize their values. It could assist them in recognizing the religious elements already present in their lives, and in discovering and responding to the implications of those elements, just as Socrates elicited responses from his students which were based on the implications of the students' own experiences.

Such an approach could help those who utilized it to make the commitment to lead a Christian life, somewhat as Augustine was prepared for his conversion to Christianity by his study of neoplatonism. It could not give anyone faith, certainly, but it might make it easier for some people to overcome the obstacles which are keeping them from accepting faith.

It is true that reason alone cannot convince anyone to adopt the Christian value system in its entirety, for Jesus taught a way of life which in some respects transcends reason and perhaps even contradicts it. Reason can demonstrate, however, that the Christian value system is more in harmony with the findings of those who have analyzed human experience down through the centuries than are hedonism, greed, and selfishness. It can plow the hard ground of at least some people's minds and hearts.

This sort of inquiry would not be a substitute for theology; it would be a preparation for it and a supplement to it. It could play a role in Christian intellectual life which no theology can possibly fill, for no theological system can substitute for a reasoned analysis of the religious significance of one's own experience.

Socrates was convinced that, if he asked the right questions, he could elicit the same responses from different people, because he was touching something universal which underlies everyone's experiences. He taught that realities are more important than appearances, that the spiritual is more important than the material, and that moral goodness is the most precious of all possessions. His followers accepted these things as true, not because Socrates had uttered them, but because he had helped them to realize for themselves that they could not be false.

Christians believe that the teachings of Jesus, no less than those of Socrates, are based upon objective reality. God does not permeate all human experience, and love is not the most perfect mode of human existence, because Jesus said that it was so: Jesus pointed out things which always had been and always will be true, but which we often find it difficult to accept or to act upon.

If it is indeed true that spiritual realities underlie all human experience and can be discovered in all human experience, then it must be possible to use the same techniques which Socrates used to show that it is true. If it is possible to find "footprints" of God in the physical world, as St. Bonaventure believed, it also should be possible to find similar evidence of the divine presence in the hundreds of acts of love and sacrifice and devotion which take place every day before our eyes.

Karl Rahner, among others, has written that God is not the conclusion to an argument but one of the presuppositions of human existence. The reality of God, in other words, already is within us, waiting to be drawn out—as it was drawn out for our friend in the restaurant, who suddenly realized that the existence of love presupposes the existence of God. This means that it must be possible to demonstrate this fact in a Socratic manner to those who do not find the traditional proofs convincing.

This approach might be especially effective in dealing with so-called "fallen-away" Catholics: those who no longer are able to believe in what they were taught as children but still are looking for something which they can believe in. In a certain sense many of these people already have taken the first step toward genuine faith, for there cannot be a true leap of faith unless there is uncertainty.

Agnostics—which simply means people who are uncertain—by definition are still searching. They are aware of what they do not know, which is the starting point in the search for wisdom. The fact that they already have taken this step should make them particularly receptive to a Christian-oriented process of Socratic inquiry.

Few people make the leap of faith from a position of contentment and security. It is those who have come to realize that there is no solid ground beneath their feet, not those who are satisfied with what they already know and believe, who are more likely to throw themselves into the outstretched arms of God.

A chain of questions which forces a person to confront the ultimate realities of human existence, such as the one which Ignatius of Loyola used with Francis Xavier, might be able to accomplish this.

Theology, on the other hand, follows faith: it does not lead one to faith, and it cannot prepare one for it.

Theology has little or nothing to say to those who have not established a true personal relationship with

God because they have not yet made the leap of faith—including those who may have come to realize, after years of living what they considered to be good Christian lives, that they never really made that leap.

Theology also cannot combat modern-day Sophism, that insidious mixture of cynicism and intellectual dishonesty which is rapidly becoming our culture's dominant ideology, and which destroys the very possibility of faith.

This is the mentality which maintains that perceptions are more important than reality: that the way to become successful, for example, is to change one's image rather than to change one's life, and that it is more important to wear the right clothes and to say the right things than it is to *do* the right things.

These are the voices which are insisting that there is nothing more to life than what can be seen or touched. They are the people who are declaring that "whoever dies with the most toys wins," and popularizing other slogans of similar profundity which often make a strong impression upon the easily impressionable.

No one can respond to the Christian message who does not believe in truth, or denies spiritual reality, or is totally self-oriented. These beliefs are radically anti-Christian, but theology cannot refute them because they deny the presuppositions upon which every theology is based.

William A. Herr

They are, however, precisely the kinds of beliefs which Socrates devoted his life to opposing and a Christian version of the Socratic midwife should be able to demonstrate that modern Sophism, like its ancient counterpart, is contradicted by the facts of everyday experience.

What we need today is a kind of Christian Socrates to guide people through the difficult process of self-inquiry, to help them to accept and respond to what they discover, and to keep them from closing their eyes to conclusions which they may find uncomfortable.

We do not need just one Christian Socrates, though; we need many of them. In a larger sense what we really need is for each of us to become a Christian Socrates.

"The unexamined life is not worth living," Socrates declared. If that was true for him, it must be even more true for those who, far from believing that they have all the answers, have only one answer, Christ—and who believe that this is an answer which makes everything else uncertain. The true Christian must constantly re-examine, challenge, and inquire.

All of us have learned many, many answers. Perhaps the time has come for us to learn some new questions, and some new ways of asking questions. Perhaps it is time for us, both as individuals and as a community, to begin the search for a truly Christian wisdom.

About the Author

WILLIAM A. HERR holds a bachelor's degree from Loyola University of Chicago and a baccalaureate, licentiate and doctorate from the Institut Superieur de Philosophie of the University of Louvain. He has taught philosophy and psychology at the college level. He is the author of *Catholic Thinkers in the Clear and This Our Church,* and his writing has also appeared in *The Critic, Ethics,* and *The Massachusetts Review.*